Bird Words

Poetic images of wild birds

Hugh David Loxdale

BRAMBLEBY BOOKS

BIRD WORDS: *Poetic images of wild birds*
Copyright© Hugh David Loxdale 2003

ISBN 0-9543347-3-6

Published 2003 by
BRAMBLEBY BOOKS,
Harpenden, Hertfordshire, UK
www.bramblebybooks.co.uk

*Cover Design by Stuart Townsend
Front cover photograph by Chris Gomersall,
Back cover photographs by Wayne Gillat and Chris Gomersall,
Author's photograph by Sinead Lynch*

Printed in Germany for Brambleby Books by
AZ Druck und Datentechnik GmbH, Kempten, Germany

BIRD WORDS

Poetic images of wild birds

Poetry by the same author:

The Eternal Quest (1988), Merlin Books Ltd.
(under the pseudonym Hugh Llewellyn);
Re-published by Brambleby Books in 2003
(under the name of Hugh David Loxdale)

Fascinating Felines (2002), Brambleby Books

Blue Skies in Tuscany (2000), Minerva Press Ltd., London
Re-published by Brambleby Books in 2003

To my nephew, Robert Allyn Davis

About the Author

Hugh Loxdale is a professional biologist and has been watching birds since an early age. He has travelled the world to observe them, in Britain and Europe, North and South America, the West Indies, Asia, Australia and the Pacific. The present selection of poems reflects the author's love of the natural world and his deep fascination with birds, their beauty and variety of form, colour and voice, as well as their complex, sometimes mysterious behaviour. Of all the species he has seen, those inhabiting Britain remain his favourites, many of which are featured here. These poems have been inspired by encounters with living wild birds in their natural habitat. This is his fourth collection of poetry. He is married and presently lives with his wife in Harpenden, Hertfordshire.

Preface

These poems were written over the period 1984 – 2003, mostly in southern England, although some were written abroad, i.e. Denmark (*Birds of Marsh and Lake, Stars in the Western Sky*); France (*Blackcap*); Bavaria, Germany (*Don't Shoot the Coot, The Black Redstart*); Arizona, USA (*Hummingbirds*); and Nevis, West Indies (*Caribbean Swallows, Frigate Birds, Music of the Finches, Pearly-Eyed Thrasher, The Cuckoo*). Most of the poems concern individual bird species, although a few are descriptions of habitat, seasons, weather, 'atmosphere', etc., and include birds as an integral part of the landscape, e.g. *Song Thrush Song*. I have enjoyed watching and listening to birds since my earliest recollections, and probably before! I thus hope that this selection may convey to the reader my continuing passion for these extraordinary creatures, co-inhabitants of our world, whose appearance, voice and behaviour, especially flight, continue to inspire. They represent a priceless gift, not only now, but also for future generations, and which therefore should be preserved along with their fragile habitats, at all cost.

The species mentioned in order of first appearance in the text include: Moorhen, *Gallinula chloropus* (17); Mallard, *Anas platyrhynchos* (17, 67); Marsh Harrier, *Circus aeruginosus* (18); Coot, *Fulica atra* (19, 30); Rough-legged Buzzard, *Buteo lagopus* (19); Reed Bunting, *Emberiza schoeniclus*; (19) House Sparrow, *Passer domesticus* (19, 63); Blackbird, *Turdus merula* (21, 59, 75) Blackcap, *Sylvia atricapilla* (22); Bullfinch, *Pyrrhula pyrrhula* (23); Barn Swallow, *Hirundo rustica* (24, 52, 73); Chiffchaff, *Phylloscopus collybita* (26, 35); Dipper, *Cinclus cinclus* (28); Wren, *Troglodytes troglodytes* (29, 60, 61); Mute Swan, *Cygnus olor* (30, 62, 80); Wood Pigeon, *Columba palumbus* (31, 75); Turtle Dove, *Streptopelia turtur* (32); Collared Dove, *Streptopelia decaocto* (32); Song Thrush, *Turdus philomelos* (32, 49, 70, 78); Mistle Thrush, *Turdus viscivorus* (32); Coal Tit, *Parus ater* (32); Marsh Tit, *Parus palustris* (32); Magnificent Frigate Bird, *Fregeta magnificens* (33); Green Woodpecker (Yaffle), *Picus viridis* (35);

Hummingbirds – Broad-Tailed, *Selasphorus platycercus*; Black-Chinned, *Archilocus alexandri*; Rivoli's, *Eugenes fulgens* (36); Sky Lark, *Alauda arvensis* (37, 47, 48); Little Tern, *Sterna albifrons* (38); Magpie, *Pica pica* (39); Starling, *Sturnus vulgaris* (40, 50, 51); Black-faced Grassquit, *Tiaris bicolor* (41); Green Parakeet, *Aratinga holochlora* (41); Peacock, *Pavo cristatus* (42); Pearly-Eyed Thrasher, *Margarops fuscatus* (43); Peregrine Falcon, *Falco peregrinus* (44); House Martin, *Delichon urbica* (44, 58, 76); Herring Gull, *Larus argentatus* (45); Swift, *Apus apus* (53, 58); Cuckoo, *Cuculus canorus* (55); Dunnock, *Prunella modularis* (57); Great Tit, *Parus major* (63); Robin, *Erithacus rubecula* (63); Kestrel, *Falco tinnunculus* (64); Wagtail, *Motacilla* sp., probably spp. *alba yarrellii* (64); Wandering Albatross, *Diomedea exulans* (65); Great Crested Grebe, *Podiceps cristatus* (68); Bittern, *Botaurus stellaris* (68); Fieldfare, *Turdus pilaris* (72); Redwing, *Turdus iliacus* (72); Black Redstart, *Phoenicurus ochruros* (76); Willow Warbler, *Phylloscopus trochilus* (76); Jay, *Garrulus glandarius* (76); Hoopoe, *Upupa epops* (76); Sparrowhawk, *Accipiter nisus* (78) .

Contents

At the Water's Edge   17

Birds of Marsh and Lake   18

Blackbird's Song   21

Blackcap   22

The Bullfinch   23

Caribbean Swallows   24

Reluctant Spring   26

Dawn Chorus   27

Dippers   28

Don't Shoot the Coot   30

Fat Wood Pigeons   31

For the Birds   32

Frigate Birds   33

Green Mood Bird and the Herald of Spring   35

Hummingbirds   36

Land of Song   37

Little Tern   38

Magpies   39

May   40

Music of the Finches   41

The Peacock   42

Pearly-Eyed Thrasher   43

Peregrine   44

Seagulls   45

Skylark 1   47

Skylark 2   48

Song Thrush Song   49

Starlings   50

Stars in the Western Sky   51

Swallows   52

Swifts   53

The Cuckoo   55

The Dunnock   57

The Gathering   58

The Known Bird (Lament for a black songster) 59

The Wren   60

The Rain and the Wrens   61

The Swan   62

At the Threshold of Spring   63

Unknown Heroes   64

Wandering Albatross   65

Weather for Ducks   67

Ode to a Great Crested Grebe   68

Bird Words?   70

Winter Visitors   72

Birds and Trees   74

Evening   75

The Black Redstart   76

The Song Thrush and the Sycamore   78

Six White Swans   80

At the Water's Edge

At the water's edge,
So wide and clear,
The yellow flags stand and wave
For pleasure and in cheer, not for pity's sake...
And the dour Moorhen with red and saffron bill,
Skulks at the sedges' base
To release a resounding cry, blood curdling shrill,
When children, nearby, play
And sport and try...
Whilst the Mallards, calm onlookers
To the human world,
Rest, huddled together on the grass,
Taking all in, a philosophical stance,
Or maybe not, and if not, wisely so,
As the huge sun sets, the foxes glow,
Or at least their eyes do,
Beyond the reed beds thick,
Waiting their chance to steal a pale green egg
Or two, or tasty duckling,
Or gaudy drake.

Birds of Marsh and Lake

Reed, rush and sedge,
A demarcation, a fringe that
Surrounds this, the edge of what is
To some a large pond, to others
Almost a lake.

And make what you will of it,
Here the birds abound.

Not that the sound, single or collective,
Can be distinctly heard
Above the wind, persistent,
Seemingly always, despite
The sun's presence.

The Marsh Harriers,
Tri-coloured male and dark chestnut
Female, glide and drift
Overhead, searching, ever searching
The ground below for signs of life,
A motion of the grass beyond
Its passive caressing
By the attentive breeze.

Sometimes they swoop down low,
To almost touch the land…and re-establish
Their awareness of its soft, waterlogged reality.

At other times, they rise up,
To wheel and swerve, to kiss
In mid-air…before falling away
To go their separate ways…

Just specks against the immensity
Of the landscape.

At the water's midst, the Coots
And ducks, ever slick, gather around
In mutual protection,
Reducing the likelihood of
Falling victim to any roving eagle eye
Nearby – or maybe just because they seek
Company and strive to be together in one place,
As humans do.

Of which is true, I cannot say, but hazard a guess...

Although I suggest that the Rough-Legged Buzzard
Atop the long dead tree, bleached and free
Of any adornments, is a better source
To find an answer.

Only at the very margins,
Near the wavering stems,
Can animate song be discerned.

At first from the confines of
A stunted willow – a strong 'zeek'...
And then a more lyrical little ditty,
Sung by the Reed Bunting,
He of striking black head and bib,
Slightly more bold and pretty
Than the old cock Sparrow...

Hunting for seeds and insect fare,
Which he gains by flying out
To the sedge heads, to cling and sing...
And then return, again and again,
In fluttering flight...
To be temporarily obscured amidst the

Moving plants, …then finally…
And terminally, lost from sight.

Blackbird's Song

Despite the lateness of spring
To arrive,
And the hastening twilight gloom
Beyond the room
In which - presently - I reside,
A Blackbird,
Quite close by,
Manages to sing
With joy unrestrained
His mellifluous cry
To cheer those locally
Whose spirits are, this day,
Like mine -
Low and drained -
Spelling out a simple theme;
Be glad; thrive
For you are still alive!
Dream not, but act
Swift against staid reality.
Then soon things should prove fine,
And nothing worthy
You desire
Along life's journey
Be denied,
But rather,
May exist in fact.

Blackcap

Alone amidst tall
Bay laurel trees,
The cock Blackcap sings long
Its exuberant, deliberate song…
Not to please
The human ear…
But to declare to rivals strong
That it sees all!

The Bullfinch

The Bullfinch,
A striking bird,
Often seen
In monogamous pairs,
Male and female with pink-red
And grey breast feathers
Respectively,
Selectively tears
At the juiciest winter buds,
Thus giving it
The status of a pest
Amongst fruit growers, gardeners
And the like.
However I notice
That come the Spring,
Hawthorn,
So severely attacked
In the cold months
December to March,
Flowers profusely as always,
Its vigour and health
Little impaired,
Suggesting the scorn
Levelled at the Bullfinch
To be, probably,
Somewhat unfair.

Caribbean Swallows

The day has done its best…
And now the sun,
Still quite bright and orange,
Sinks rapidly below the waves
Of a tropical Caribbean sea,
More grey than blue.

Flocks of Swallows,
Several dozen strong,
As silent as ghosts,
Fly swiftly past,
Up and down the beach…
So low that they almost
Stroke the clipped grass
At its upper reach
With their streamlined wings.

Where have they been?
Where are they going?

Since they now have no voice,
We cannot utter a question to them,
We can muse and sing,
Shout loudly in the air,
But they are not saying
What their purpose is, nor their goal,
As they swoop and dance
Above the relentless tide.

Probably they are feasting here
En route to more southern climes.

All that can be said for certain
Is that their little lives
Are immeasurably tougher than ours,
Their quest more pressing,
Their adventure more arduous -
And audacious.

They should be saluted...
Though the people of the sand,
Only see their ball, their game,
A transient bandying
Of a coloured sphere, soft and pleasant,
Whereas to the birds,
The world is their plaything,
And the magnitude of their migration,
And its strangeness,
Their eternal secret.

Reluctant Spring

Today, at last, the reluctant Spring
Yielded to the sun;
Mid-April's warmth,
Checking a chill north breeze,
Releasing Brimstones
From their long respite
And making
The flowering Sallows
Hum with frantic bees.
Yet still the Chiffchaff's voice delays;
That small, sonorous, monotone bird,
Bold claimant to the woodland air,
Whilst except for insects, Sallow
And of course,
Celandine in bright displays,
Most else remains
Serene and bare;
An unawakened source
Of beauty.

Dawn Chorus

Even before first light has broken,
The birds in the wood have awoken
And with harmonious words, each spoken
Of their rights to the space - they say -
Is theirs;
A beauteous token gesture,
Prelude to a new spring day.

Dippers

Fierce peat-stained waters
Rushing loudly,
Sent into turbulent flow
Through a constriction;
Big moss-covered boulders,
A natural funnel.
Peculiarly gnarled and twisted
Oak and beech,
Wearing dowdy
Lichens from branch and twig,
Flanking each river bank
To form a tunnel,
Their shading limbs
Sometimes bent
Downwards
Touching the very water's
Surface,
Or reaching below.
A flash of brilliant white
Amidst the otherwise sombre light.
'Look, over there, a Dipper!'
'Where?'
'There, standing on the smaller
Of the two large rocks
Guarding the mouth of the race.'
'I can't see it.'
'Oh yes, I see it, and look -
Another to the right
Beyond the first,
Half-immersed.'
Soon both Dippers are together,
Completely high and dry

On the same rock.
Bobbing, active,
Medium-sized brown birds,
With sharp bill,
Short tail and wide pale breast,
Not dissimilar in profile
To a Wren.
Suddenly,
They spot us
And within an instant,
Take off,
Flying low upstream,
Past the disused mill
On the bend
Until out of sight.
At this point,
We return the three miles
Or so along the wooded track
To the parked car and lunch.
As I go back,
My thoughts are mixed:
Initially pleased
I have at last seen
These fine birds,
Then slowly becoming
Uncomfortable and unsure,
An instinctive feeling of loss -
A hunch
I might never
See them again,
Either as individuals,
Nor the species;
That this is to be
The one and only occasion
Our narrowing paths
Are actually
To cross.

Don't Shoot the Coot

Please don't shoot
The Coot;
It's a nice bird really…
With its sleek black livery
And snowy cap…
Bobbing gently on the lake;
Occasionally submerging
To take a piece
Of stringy weed…
To satisfy a hungry need.

Its voice is not very musical;
Not at all like a flute…

More of a car horn
As it sounds off,
Shrilly about
Territory and mate.

Certainly compared
With the grey swans
Upturned nearby,
It is rarely, if ever,
So mute.

Fat Wood Pigeons

Two fat Wood Pigeons
On the lawn
Feed hurriedly
Trying fast
To gain another ounce
Ever wary
Of men with guns
Ready to blast,
Or the cat in the hedge
With claws drawn
Ready to pounce.
Soon they fly off -
Perhaps to cabbages,
Perhaps to wheat;
Welcome and unwelcome dinner guests;
Beautiful pink-grey birds:
To some - a wondrous treat,
To others - nothing but hated pests.

For the Birds
(To Christopher)

May you...be able to
Tell a Turtle
From a Collared Dove,
Flying in the heavens
Blue above.

A Song...
From a Mistle Thrush
That both sit on high
And sing...
Gladly before the rush
Of urgent dawn.

And yet once,
A Coal
From the fawn Marsh Tit,
Hanging from a bough,
Whose words are oft scolding,
But beautiful...
And true.

Frigate Birds

A pirates' circle,
Danced by a solitary pair
In the heavy turbulent air
Above a tropic sea.

A bird of immense grace,
Almost beauty, certainly skill,
Weaving and swooping
To pick up a fish
On the meniscus;

To chase seabirds of another kind,
To make them yield
Their prize
Against their will;

Or to follow the small
Fishing boats that ply
These shallow waters,
Hoping for a throwaway
To act as lunch.

Their wings are long and black;
Their beaks and tails long too;
The latter deeply forked.

Despite all this excellence,
This streamlined perfection,
There is something vampiric
About them, -

Their silence, their rapaciousness,
Though piratical is probably the
Best adjective.

Either way, they make me
Shudder to see them,
Whilst wondering in awe.

No doubt the birds
That they harass,
Feel likewise about them,
And very fast... withdraw.

Green Mood Bird and the Herald of Spring

Again and again the Yaffle cries,
Penetrating clear April skies:
A cruel and mocking laugh
To disquiet the sturdiest heart -
Or soul,
Treading the muddy path
That skirts the lake,
Ever looking for hope, peace, contentment
Some good goal
From which purpose
One can make.
Then at last, a Chiffchaff sang,
The Yaffle stopped, then began,
Then stopped once more -
Surprised, no doubt, as I was
By the rightness
Of those clipped words,
Produced by the drabbest
Of all drab birds -
Fear not, they spoke,
Spring is here.

A total rout.

Hummingbirds

Here on Mount Lemmon's*
Higher peaks,
Where now,
The wind only occasionally
Speaks through fir and pines,
The contents of nature's jewel box
Have been spilled...
Those little animate specks
That have thrilled
Many a passer-by...
Including myself...
The hummingbirds...
Adorned in brilliant hues,
With glittering feathers...
Of green, purple, black and red...
Their long beaks
Piercing the forest flowers...
And then, in an instant,
Gone...at the blink of an eye...
Back to the cloudless sky
And the dark wooded edge...
An illusion of the purest kind...
One that haunts the mind...
And inspires the question:
'Was what I saw true?'...
Here on the lonely
Peaks of Mount Lemmon,
Halfway up towards Heaven,
Where these tiny angels dwell.

* Arizona, USA

36

Land of Song

In a place just west of Broadbalk*,
Where the wind blows keen and strong,
The Skylarks defend their sacred plots
With a wealth of miraculous song.

Up, up they rise so high,
Stopping at every 'floor',
Singing their little hearts out,
Singing all the more.

Full five minutes they often last,
Repeating every phrase,
Tiny specks below the clouds,
Singing out their days.

At length they slowly descend to earth,
To parachute...and then to flop,
Singing yet for all their worth,
Until within the crop.

The energy, the urgency
That powers their flight from ground,
A defiance of all boundaries,
To fill the sky with sound.

We hardly know and cannot see
Any visible fence or line,
And only halt enraptured
Since their voice is so divine.

* Rothamsted estate, Harpenden, Hertfordshire

Little Tern

Flying low over a wave-lashed spit
Into cold wind
And trailing spray,
Rude enough
To make the hardiest
Rambler
Shudder and glance away,
The Little Tern,
Epitome of grace and beauty,
Pushes steadily on
Without concern.
White bird of slender wings and forked tail
Seeming to our eyes, incredibly frail,
But suited perfectly to its arduous life-
A rugged spirit enduring bleak inlet bay,
Sandbank and coastal waters rife.

Magpies

To us,
Such sorrow as
A Magpie may bring,
Is for small birds,
A very real thing,
Whilst two, a pair,
With young in the nest,
Is no joy, but a double curse
Since to feed their offspring,
They rob the neighbours
Even worse.

May

The strongest impression
Made upon me
This May
Is not
The contrast between
The beauty of chestnut flowers
And their disappointing smell,
Countless buttercups
Strewn in loose array
Over wet meadow
And grassy vale,
Nor the jet black
Saint Mark's flies
Swarming, with dangling legs,
Low in thundery skies.
But, curiously enough
These past few weeks,
That of juvenile Starlings,
Now everywhere -
On branches, ground, railings -
Begging with impatient screeching cries
And flapping wings
In order to catch
Parental ears and eyes;
Then gaping wide
As experienced beaks
Cram down further supplies;
Frequently, more of the same blessed insects,
No longer a tasty surprise
To these fast growing,
Decidedly drab young things.

Music of the Finches

The Grassquits
On the hammock strings play,
Jumping between lines
On the fan-shaped array.
The music though is not of a harp, -
Of Saint-Saëns or Mathias
In C or C-sharp.

Nor of those reptilian notes
From the cold Blue Lias,
Echoing down epochs
Without diminution or bias.

The music is rather
A prolonged kiss,
Between black-faced male
And dowdy female;
Who share a love,
As a dove might do
Or indulgent Green Parakeets...
Which they never miss,
Or rarely,
Being seen mostly in pairs,
So that at the heartstrings
The message always tears.

The Peacock

The Peacock,
Noble bird
As observed from its raised crest,
Royal blue breast
And splendid trailing tail
Studded with emerald rings
In the male,
Has now been reduced
At the zoo
To scavenging crumbs
Dropped by the many
Who come to view
Such creatures
In an unnatural state.
How I hate to see true
Majesty thus fallen.
Much better, for sure
Is this creature home
Amidst the tangled jungles
East, or stately strutting the lawns
Centuries of western culture have
Produced;
That most manicured bequest,
Once the strange delight
Solely of lords and kings.

Pearly-Eyed Thrasher

The Pearly-Eyed Thrasher,
A large brown thrush-like bird,
Came and had lunch with us today,
Though uttered not a word.

It perched on a chair back
And studied us with its gaze;
A deep and translucent eye it had
With a glistening, pearly glaze.

We threw it crumbs of bread to eat,
But it made not a move,
Contemplating our every thought,
Until our intentions we could prove.

Finally it swooped to earth,
To snatch our little gift,
Then flew straight back to the forest;
A power to fast uplift.

Peregrine

Beyond the resolve
Of the human eye,
A Peregrine sits,
But will not fly...
On a cliff ledge,
Inaccessibly high,
Far from earth
And near the sky.

With sleek, slate wings
And white, grained breast...
It waits a further while
To complete its rest...
Until the Martins
Which gracefully swoop...
Are oblivious
To the loop,
The arc
That it transcends...
Now straight - as a bullet...

That ends
With a strike!

And a lone feather,
Which descends
To the ground...
Silent...
Without sound...
Above the rolling sea...
And a distant, mewing
Cry.

Seagulls

With the racing November sky -
Sunlit and stormy -
A swirling backcloth
Of purple-black
Rent, at times, to reveal
Seams of deep azure,
Five Seagulls,
Contrasted white and pure,
Ride the flustered air -
Their long wings
Held alternately flexed, then straight -
Whilst they dive, soar and bank
Fast above
Dank, empty fields.
Silent and menacing,
Like the dark clouds,
Few small birds stir or sing
When, with thin shadows fleeting thrown,
These powerful marauders from the coast
Pass by
Looking for easy fare.
Majestic, streamlined, keen-eyed, stern,
At sea, a respectable living they mostly earn,
Searching the wave-tops, pools and wrack
For marine morsels
On which to feed...
Whereas in winter, far inland,
Away from cold salt spray and heaving sand,
A more dubious life then they lead,
Following the plough
For the hapless worm,
Or worse -

Rummaging rubbish tips -
Vile and rank -
For scraps of food;
The much-appreciated waste
From city and town.

Skylark 1

Glad bird of the wide blue yonder,
Often have I stopped to ponder,
And look toward that speck up high,
Lost link between earth and sky.

No bough or branch does he require,
Only the lofty stars does he aspire,
To cling and sing at the edge of space,
And claim his throne and jibe his race.

Skylark 2

I hear the Lark's distant song
Carried on the wind…
High up, below the threatening clouds
It hovers, blameless…and without sin.

Song Thrush Song

Hidden amongst
Hawthorn brush
Clothing a distant ridge
Or high up, perhaps,
In an Ash tree,
Old and tall,
Whose stately silhouette
Is poetry itself,
The Song Thrush -
In fine voice and feather -
Bewails us all
This late Spring
With its melodious cry;
A stark collection of tunes -
Both ecstatic and plaintive -
Intermixed:
A song
At once
Too ethereal and wry
To wholly enjoy,
And yet,
I myself,
Like many,
Would be the poorer
Were it and its speckled composer
Suddenly,
And forever,
Gone.

Starlings

Starlings by chill winds blown,
Loose flocks like dark seeds sown,
Alighting amidst tangled thorns,
Or sometimes upon uncut lawns;
Black specks that spill and waft...
In contrast, the light snow flecks
Travelling straight - and determined
Astride the raw east's draught -
Both drawn to this,
The March wind's home;
A picture, clear of warmth
As lost summers,
Now none too bright,
Once shot in monochrome.

*Stars in the Western Sky**

The Stars in the western sky
Fly a great flock,
Each a black cross, silhouetted,
Locked into a rigid, silent grid,
Veering, swirling as smoke,
In concert, a crystal lattice,
At once a figure of eight,
Against the disturbed,
Rain-filled clouds.

They mock our notions
Of coordination,
Of an understanding of nature...
And pass on...to disappear
Beyond the hill
And the church's exposed, bell-clad
Spire. An enigma remaining
Of which, I for one, never tire.

*In German, Starling (*Sturnus vulgaris*) = Star

Swallows

A lovely shining purple sheen,
The Swallows of the evening scene
Follow close the contours in the dunes;
A sinusoidal frenzy,
Silent, bereft of the many tunes
They know by heart,
Learnt around the cowsheds and farmyards
From their parents' mouths
Before the start
Of their immense journey south -
And back.
A miracle yet that they are here now,
Built to hawk and wing,
And catch a fly...
And dispel, disperse the lie...
That they are God's chosen ones -
Just restless spirits
Vying for life
Across the sands of Sylt*.

*Largest island off northern Germany

Swifts

The aerial spectacle,
Begun in May,
Continues throughout June, July
And on into August
In the clear pastel skies
Above town and English countryside;
Slick, curved black shapes,
Perfect designs
To cut and scythe
The sunlit air,
They swoop down -
Single, in formation or in line -
With effortless speed and grace,
Rolling, twisting, occasionally shrill screaming
As they come to distribute death
Amongst the tiny, winged multitudes below.

But these are not the Spitfires, Hurricanes
Or Messerschmitts of old,
And the destruction they cause
Not the vengeance of a cruel war.
Rather, a perennial struggle
To feed, reproduce
And fly free again.
One that, maybe, will never end -
Assuming the Spring and they return -
Year after year,
Long into the unimagined future,
Beyond human strife and bombs,
So that this most joyous scene shall remain,
The Swifts in full chase or play,
A certainty, a must

Each May
And on into August.

The Cuckoo

The Cuckoo,
Under an innocent sky,
Skulks in the bushes
To study me...
Its striped breast tantalising...
And its long grey tail, -
Its stares unmoved
With a yellow eye,
Like a basilisk
To strike me dead...
Were my curiosity
As large as its...
To get the better of me,
Enough to approach
Closer still;
To fill
The field of vision;
To pry
Into the soul
Of this exotic bird
Of the forest...
A parasite true,
One of exquisite beauty...
That a birder would
Eagerly tick,
But to its neighbours
Is a sight to make
Them fully sick...
A creature unloved
By the many, -
Who must fulfil its
Destiny, whatever,

Its mission to lie,
As it seeks the world,
And its next victims,
Its huge, unpleasant chick
So adorable,
That few parents
Can deny.

The Dunnock
(*Prunella modularis*)

Prunella is as Prunella does,
The drabbest bird that ever was,
Only its song exceeds all joy,
So much its rivals does it annoy.

Hiding in the shrubbery thick,
Or singing from a favoured stick,
But never a female underrate,
For she has more than a single mate.

To cavort and frolic in ecstasy,
To rear her brood, half for free,
Her dutiful husband does she so dupe,
A dirty trick (perhaps) to which to stoop.

The Gathering

In a shallow valley
Cut by the River Ver*,
The Swifts make great gathering
And there the dead air stir.

They fly with rapid wing beats
And mark this summer's course,
Swooping, wheeling and diving,
An impressive single force.

But in-between the silence
And screams of raucous joy,
Come the lyrical strains and twitters
That Martins glad deploy.

So that this large flock
Is not homogeneous, each and every one,
Beneath the searching cumulus
That tease the brilliant sun.

All about, and everywhere
The birds enact their play,
Then suddenly, as they appeared,
Are gone…without delay.

* Hertfordshire

The Known Bird
(Lament for a black songster)

The Blackbird,
In jettest black
Who, six months prior,
Thrilled the Spring skies
With its matchless voice,
Now lies stilled
In the mouth
Of a pretty Cat,
Not out of choice...
Mainly bad luck.

One cannot condemn
The skilled hunter...
It is her prerogative
And desire.
Although I do decry
The bird.
That vision
Who brought such joy
And became complacent
To danger...
Which is a tragedy...
And our loss too...
That beautiful, guileless creature...
Never again
To be heard.

The Wren

The Wren - ubiquitous, energetic, shrill,
Fills the March woodlands
With its exuberant trill.
What an irrepressible avian sprite,
This chestnut bird
With upturned tail
And a lot of nerve -
Challenging all
With its might!

The Rain and the Wrens

It rained quite heavily last night...
I know, because I can see its residue;
Shining, glistening like dew
On the lip of cowslip and bluebell,
Yet to be warmed by the morning sun.

I can see the wetness on the ground
And the river's spate too;
Flowing and singing its gurgling, mesmeric song
Beneath the bridge...and someway beyond...

Whilst grey, sullen clouds
Try to break ranks...and let the sunshine through...
Even as the bumblebees
Do what they have to do,
(And this despite the morning's chill).

Nearby, the Wrens in shrill duet
Hop; they must from branch to branch,
Almost unseen in the bright Forsythia bush,
Staking their claim of recognition
Before this spring day's rush
Begins, as we have always loved it
And indeed, once knew.

The Swan

Upon
Still waters
Fed
By the River Gade*,
A pure white Swan -
Mute unless angry -
Glides gently
Along its course,
Once dipping
Near the bank
To pause
And see
If I possess
Bread
To give it.
Regrettably, I do not
And am hungry
Myself…
So we part quickly,
I, at least,
Having something
To thank
For this brief encounter;
A close view
Of perfection.

* Hertfordshire

At the Threshold of Spring

Above the incessant traffic noise
The cold March wind
Is just discerned
To whisper with muffled voice
As it plays nonchalantly
Amongst bare Poplar twigs
Whose sharp buds have hardly yet awoke.
So too, sometimes,
Can the Sparrows' chirps be heard,
The Great Tit's strident double call,
Plus the Robin's fluid song -
A bird
Uttering delicate, rippling notes,
Now at the threshold of Spring -
To exclaim the sanctity of his estate
And recount his virtues to a fastidious mate.
Meanwhile,
Masses of low cloud -
A fascinating wash of white and greys -
Course quiescent across the blue sky,
These last few days
From east to west;
One vast, invading force;
A splendid sight to watch,
Like life itself,
Persistent, but equally as
Unknowing in the eternal quest.

Unknown Heroes

Above scorched autumnal fields,
A Kestrel swoops on mouse or vole.

When it rises…unsuccessful…
It is not alone
Being mocked by small birds,
Wagtails probably,
Kind unknown.

Two in particular,
Bravest of the brave,
Persist in the attack,
Following every nuance,
Dive and veer,
Like air aces of long ago,
Defiant against a superior foe.

Surprisingly, the hunter
Eventually yields
To their lack
Of fear
And moves away…
Leaving two indistinguishable specks…
Victors
Of the day.

Wandering Albatross

Slender companion of the arching winds,
How stiff you ride the truculent gale
On long wings;
How you glide
Just above the water's grasp,
The deep turquoise,
Split by milk-white spume,
Torn to shreds by the frigid, rampant air...

You pace on relentlessly,
Coasting, veering, steering
Your rapid course home.
Never a glance backwards
Across the empty vastness
Of the southern seas.

Lonely, so lonely, you ply
This strange odyssey.
What do you consider all
These empty hours,
When even sleep is snatched
Between the troughs of huge swells?

What inspires you when you awake,
To focus on the shifting, unruly
Clouds above, the weak sun obscured,
Fog, the crescent moon,
Or the awesome, incomprehensible
Field of stars?...

On you wing your way,
Traverse the near endless miles,

Round the globe…
To test its endurance,
And its rotundity…

And then, one day,
Perhaps brilliant April green, -
The strong pastel light formed
In the east as the sun awakes,
Land is seen.

At first, faintly, shadowy, obscure.
Later, as the minutes slip by,
With the wind rustling past
Your crisp feathers of wing and tail,
Less distant, more solid.

An island, an amorphous rock
Protruding unique above
The flatness of the horizon.
Land of your birth,
Half a century before,
And land too of your mate,
Many days since last seen.
Guardian of that large cream pearl
In its strange raised nest;
Investment for your kind…
And all our futures…

Our legacy, yet a paradox;
As hopeless in its geometry
As a spent bullet,
Soon it will hatch,
Ultimately to yield
A being that even the Gods must surely envy…
Except for its prolonged, solitary wanderings.

Weather for Ducks

The weather
Is in an emotional state
This afternoon.

Sunshine at lunch;
Torrential rain by teatime.
It is still quite sunny,
But a large metallic grey
Cloud now hangs over us;
Dominating us
And our plans
To walk home...
Or to the pub...
Whichever is dearer.

No doubt the
Four Mallard ducks
On the River Lea
By the bridge,
Shining green and blue,
Will not mind
Even if it does rain
Again.

When you are that soaked
Already
What is a little more
From heaven.
A divine blessing indeed
For them,
And a mixed one
For us.

Ode to a Great Crested Grebe

You fantastic bird!
Ruby-red of eye, perilous of beak,
Bifurcated black 'punk' hair
With a wide parting,
And chestnut and black 'beard':
A marvellous head perched on a long neck
And rounded, squat body.
A most incredible assemblage of
Form and design,
As outrageous as any that
Parisian Haute Couture could
Surely conceive;
Indeed the height of fashion.
Necessary too as you display
Your beauty, scoot upright across the water
On your lobed feet in parallel display
With an intended mate;
To swap strands of stringy weed...
And maybe thence to breed,
Lay some eggs in a damp, floating nest
Of aquatic plants and twigs;
Rear zebra striped chicks
So bold, that on your back are carried.
You are a dream come true.
A gorgeous creature –
Whether by God's design or Darwin's random walk,
No one can divine your existence
Let alone, encapsulate the strangeness
Of your being,
Adrift on those deep, empty lakes
Where, at the periphery,
Only the elusive Bittern, twice shy at least,

Staves off loneliness by its
Booming cry,
But cannot match you in
Terms of sheer wondrousness.

Bird Words?*

Georgie, Georgie, Georgie, Georgie, Georgie.
Hello, Hello, Hello!
I know you're there!

Where are you, where are you,
Where are you, where are you?
Are you all right?...

Coward......coward...
Phew! Phew! Phew!

Look, look, look, look, look,
Look, look, look, look...
I am not frightened...of you
You know that, you know that.

You're a lunatic, you're a lunatic, lunatic, lunatic.

We know, we know, we know, we know, we know...
Show yourself, show yourself, show yourself...
You creep, creep, creep, creep, creep, cree-up...

You're just, just, just, just, just...
A peewit...ha, ha, ha, ha, ha!
You're cheap, cheap.
Look, look, look, look, look, look, look...
You all right? You all right? You all right?
You all right? You all right?...

Look at me..., me..., meeee...
I can see you, see you, I can see you.
We know, we know, we know, we know.

Lunatic, lunatic.
Ha, ha, ha, ha, ha!
Creep, cheap, cheap, cheap, cheap.
Flutey, fruity, fruity, fruity.
Where, where?…

Georgie, Georgie, Georgie, Georgie, Georgie.
Wake up, wake up, wake up…
Brrrrh! Cheer up, cheer up, cheer up, cheer up!
Creep, creep, creep, creep.
You can nev…er win…cha, cha, cha.

We know, we know, we know, we know.
Give up, give up,
Creep, creep.
You son of a …cha, cha, cha.

Sink, sink, sink, sink, sink, sink,
You, you, you, you…
Why don't you…give in!
Give up, give up, give up, give up, give up, give up,
Georgie! Georgie! Georgie!

Wake up, wake up, wake up,
Where are you, where are you?
Look at me…Zzzrrr!

You lunatic, you lunatic, lunatic, lunatic.
Go home, go home, go home, go home.

Shout, shout, shout, shout, shout, shout, shout, shout,
Look at me, me, meee…e!

Are you still there…Georgie?

*The voice of a Song Thrush, singing high up in a Sycamore tree.

Winter Visitors

In early March
On days like this -
Dull and overcast,
Now some weeks past -
The Fieldfares and Redwings went,
Though exactly whereabouts
I do not know -
Most left too fast.
Of those I saw go,
Many seemed to fly north-east,
Whilst others,
In wispy flocks,
Flew around a great circuit
Chattering
Above the bleak, wide field,
Since Christmas
Their windswept home,
To land awhile in excited rest.
Then, once more,
To take flight
With renewed zest
And head on -
Which-ways till lost from sight;
Small, flitting
Silhouettes
Against the ruffled sky.
One wonders why
These handsome birds,
Hopping with assured ease,
Or singing untunefully
Without reproach
In scraggy trees,

Find it necessary
To leave this steady land
For another course
And face uncertain
Times abroad.
Where - or whatever it is
The attractive force
Pulling them far away,
I do not want to follow.

Instead,
Whilst I miss their leaving,
I'll last here - half-believing -
That some other kinds
May soon arrive
On a sunnier day,
For one,
The glistening Swallow,
To enchant
And then also,
Eventually,
To depart;
As with estranged lovers,
A power to deprive.

Birds and Trees

Trees equals birds;
Birds equals trees;
Thus few trees equals fewer birds;
And fewer birds equals fewer trees
Still. Equals (ultimately)...a desert.

Evening

On May the twenty third, as the day,
Once so hot and lusty, subsides into cool reflection,
The distant cirrus, bathed in pale gold sunlight,
Transcend into tranquil stasis, and the boys,
Once so noisy, end their play,
To retire to dinner, the reactions of life
Are not quite stilled.

Even as the clock strikes eight, the Blackbirds
Astride the roof tops, silhouetted and cocky,
Strike up their own alarm; a cascade of
Reciprocated calls, strident, insensitive, uncaring
Of the small black bees that still ply their trade
Amidst the purple geranium's lure -
That pureness of colour, beheld in the
Emperor's wings, his mirrored cloak.

The pigeons make haste to court and mate...
They rustle with hard flapping feathers at the lilac's crown...
Though with the receding light, calm is soon restored...
A melody of restraint,
With Blackbird and doves all
Around, tempering the silence
With their liquid song...

Night steals in to reign supreme...
All knowing night, a purveyor of uncertainty,
To bandy our senses between the seen,
And unseen, heard and unheard, touched, yet untouched...
Whilst the starlit emptiness above stretches to infinity...
And considered thought is held hostage...to awe.

The Black Redstart

Finally the sun comes out and now shines
With all is trembling might...as the clouds,
Once so bold and rainy, withdraw east across the lake
To sanctuary.

The Martins again cut the air, an aeroplane drones a long way off,
Water drips from the sullen roof...and the Black Redstart
Reclaims her tangled throne...

This a gnarled apple tree, fifty years old,
Centre of the garden and our lives,
She strives to retain dominance,
Swooping down now and again
To catch an insect,
Or stare at us with her unstinting gaze.

The day moves on. A Willow Warbler recounts
Its summery song from the trees beyond the house.
The pines sway and rustle in the breeze, as does the large ash
further still.

If a Jay or stylish Hoopoe were to land on the lawn
It would gain notice, applause, respect.

Yet the Black Redstart's comings and goings are hardly heeded.
Sometimes she sits on the veranda near us, but a few feet away.
Her tameness though reflects naivety, not trust.

How can she know the true nature of reality...and by the time she
does, including the neighbour's cat lurking in the hedge,
It may be too late.

Life is an odd thing.

That the presence of a small, dark bird
With a rust-red tail can brighten an otherwise mostly dull day...
And bring joy where greater entertainments sadly fail.

Then the bird disappears with the return of the rains,
And the sun fades once more behind the veil
Of drifting clouds.

The Song Thrush and the Sycamore

It was the pulpit from which he sang,
From which joyous melody swelled and rang,
The lofty perch on which he stayed,
In those times of sun and wind…and gently swayed
To the music in the breeze…and his own
Fine notes and song, dialogue, long passages of thought,
Well conceived, but now lost…
Tossed generously into the stirring air,
Amidst the dawn chorus and his unrelenting stare,
As he looked down from this his golden throne –
A 'Throne of Kings' –
To listen, await enthralled, at what fortune brings –
A rival, a mate…or Sparrowhawk, swift and grey,
Stooping in silence upon its distracted prey.

Now though, all this is conjecture, mere speculation,
Past history; it is too late…
For the tree was felled from its high estate…
And where on sunlit boughs, a voice did soar,
To the woodpile was carried…the sycamore!
A mighty tree grown tall to perfection,
Spanned earth and sky in one straight section…
Yet so, a whole piece of trunk remains
(As witness and testimony – like that block
Awaiting the axeman's raised hand…)
A just rebuke for those who would chase…
The noble thrush from its lawful place.
And still he sits and strides the clean-cut stump,
Like a colossus in thoughts and deeds;
He does not retreat…but
Glides down, continues from the sad lump
To smack and knock an unwary snail;

A moral victory of sorts, so no defeat.
This brilliant bird, not spotless,
Though blameless, for sure…
Since his song is both blessed…and undeniably pure.

Six White Swans

Six white Swans in grace
Upon the mirrored Ammersee*,
They swim in line in ordered pace,
Serene and with dignity.

Who is the parent, who the child
Is assumed with uncertainty
As they drift along in single file
To fulfil their destiny.

Soon they pass out of sight
Towards the western shore,
As we dine and await the night
They alas are seen no more.

As morning mists clear the waters
However they reappear again in line,
Father, mother, sons and daughters;
A majestic sight before nine.

Shimmering images, now twelve,
Like the Apostles in perfection,
They bend their long necks to delve
Below that cool reflection.

*Bavaria, southern Germany